CHALLENGE AND CHANGE

Saving the Family Farm

By Ann Rossi

Illustrated by James Rownd

Picture Credits
6 (map) © National Geographic Society; 7 (top to bottom) © Gordon R. Gainer/Corbis, © Phil Schermeister/Corbis, © Mark Peterson/Corbis; 19, 27, 37, 45, 52 (diary art) David Cabot; 53 © James P. Blair/Corbis; 54 (top to bottom) © Digital Vision/Getty Images, © Bohemian Nomad Picturemakers/Corbis; 56 © Bill Ross/Corbis.

Produced through the worldwide resources of the National Geographic Society, John M. Fahey, Jr., President and Chief Executive Officer; Gilbert M. Grosvenor, Chairman of the Board; Nina D. Hoffman, Executive Vice President and President, Books and Education Publishing Group.

Prepared by National Geographic School Publishing
Ericka Markman, Senior Vice President and President, Children's Books and Education Publishing Group; Steve Mico, Senior Vice President, Publisher, Editorial Director; Francis Downey, Executive Editor; Richard Easby, Editorial Manager; Bea Jackson, Director of Design; Cindy Olson, Art Director; Margaret Sidlosky, Director of Illustrations; Matt Wascavage, Manager of Publishing Services; Lisa Pergolizzi, Sean Philpotts, Production Managers, Ted Tucker, Production Specialist.

Manufacturing and Quality Control
Christopher A. Liedel, Chief Financial Officer; Phillip L. Schlosser, Director; Clifton M. Brown, Manager.

Editors
Barbara Seeber, Mary Anne Wengel

Book Development
Morrison BookWorks LLC

Book Design
Steven Curtis Design

Art Direction
Dan Banks, Project Design Company

Published by the National Geographic Society
1145 17th Street, N.W.
Washington, D.C. 20036-4688

ISBN: 0-7922-5859-2

2015 2014 2013
 2 3 4 5 6 7 8 9 10 11 12 13 14 15

Printed in Mexico

Contents

The Peterson Family

The Peterson family lives in Ohio. They own a dairy farm. It is hard for the Petersons to make a living on their small farm. Larger farms in the area can sell milk at a low price. It is hard for

Eva

Eva is 12 years old. She enjoys writing in her diary and being outside. She enjoys working on the farm and spending time with her family.

Ingrid

Ingrid is Eva's older sister. She is studying business in college and hopes to find a way to make the family farm more profitable.

Ryan

Ryan is Eva's older brother. He helps out on the farm during his breaks from college.

small farms to compete with the large farms. Many small farms have been forced to close down. The Petersons are facing these problems when an unexpected tragedy occurs.

Kathy

Kathy is Eva's mom. She works as a teacher to help make enough income for the family to survive.

Russ

Russ is Eva's dad. He runs the family farm and works hard to keep it a profitable business.

The Midwest

This story takes place in the Midwest region of the United States. This region extends from North Dakota to Kansas and east to Ohio. The Midwest is an important farming region.

WESTERN STATES

- North Dakota
- South Dakota
- Nebraska
- Kansas

- Minnesota
- Iowa
- Missouri
- Wisconsin

- Illinois
- Indiana
- Michigan
- Ohio

The Climate

Summers in the Midwest are warm and sunny. The region gets rain all year round. Winters are usually cold with large amounts of snow.

The Location

The Midwest is in the central part of the United States. The land is either flat or has rolling hills. It is the only area in the United States with no mountain ranges. There are many large rivers and about 48,000 lakes.

The Economy

Farming is a major industry in the Midwest. There are many farms. Crops, such as wheat and corn are grown. Cattle are raised for milk and meat. The region also has iron mines and steel mills. Factories make many products such as automobiles.

A Season of Change

"That's it, I'm done!" said Eva as she spread fresh straw in the last stall in the row.

Happily, she looked over at her older sister, her blue eyes sparkling. "Do you need any help, Ingrid?"

"Nope. That was the last one for me, too," answered Ingrid as she entered the stall where Eva was working. She and Eva looked almost like twins. They had the same fair skin and blonde hair. Ingrid was the older and more serious Peterson daughter, as careful as Eva was eager.

Ingrid straightened up and leaned on her shovel. "Whew! It'll take me a while to get used to mucking out stalls every morning before breakfast again. It's one thing I definitely don't miss when I'm away at college."

"But don't you miss the smell of the barn and the fresh, sweet hay? I would. I'd miss the cows, too," Eva said as they left the cool barn and stepped into the bright sunshine. Eva looked around her from the old barn to the fenced-in **paddock.** She looked out at the herd of cows lazily grazing in the fields in the distance. "In fact," she said looking back at her sister, "I'd miss this whole place. Don't you ever miss this when you're away at school?"

"Of course I do. It's home," said Ingrid.

They climbed the worn steps to the back porch of the farmhouse with its peeling paint and patched roof. They left their shoes in the mudroom before going into the kitchen. Ryan and Mom were making breakfast.

"It's good to have you two home for the summer," said Dad to Ryan and Ingrid when everyone was seated at the breakfast table.

----

paddock – an enclosed area used for pasturing animals

"I'll say," said Eva. "The chores get done much faster with everybody helping out. Since we got the barn chores done early, can we pack a picnic and go to the pond?"

"Dad and I are going to start scraping the house so we can paint it," said Ryan.

"Can't you wait until tomorrow?" asked Eva.

"Well, Pumpkin, we have to take advantage of the good weather," said Dad. Eva looked at her father. She was proud to have such a strong, hard-working dad. His active life on the farm kept him in very good shape, and his smile always cheered her. But today she wanted him to be a little less energetic.

"But we hardly ever get to do fun stuff as a family now that Ingrid and Ryan are in college. Last week you and Ryan were so busy mowing and **baling.** Can't we take a break and do something together like we used to?" begged Eva.

"Well, maybe we can work until noon or so," said Dad. "It's going to be a hot day. It would be good to cool off this afternoon, before we start the second round of milking."

baling – collecting wheat or hay into bundles

"If the girls help me weed the garden before it gets too hot," said Mom, "then we'll pack a lunch and go to the pond. We can afford one afternoon off."

"All right!" crowed Eva, getting up from the table. "I'll start weeding right now."

Soon Eva was working her way through rows of beans and cucumbers. As the sun rose higher, Eva worked faster. Eva looked over at Mom and Ingrid. Each of them was working in a section of the garden. Dad and Ryan were scraping paint from the house. Eva breathed deeply. She smelled the rich soil, the perfume of flowers, and the sweet smells of cattle and grasses.

"It's a great day to be outside," said Mom.

"Summertime! I'm glad we all have the summers off," said Eva. "Don't you wish every day were like this?" asked Eva, smiling at her mom, who was now working in the row next to her. "We have everything here: fields, pastures, woods, and even a pond. I'm going to stay here forever. I'm going to keep farming, just like you and Dad."

"I'm glad you love the farm, Eva," her mom said, "but sometimes farming doesn't bring in enough money to pay the bills." Her gray eyes had the same serious look as Ingrid's.

"Was that why you became a teacher?" asked Eva.

Mom sighed. "Dad and I grew up on dairy farms. All we ever wanted to do was have one of our own. But then the price of milk started to go down. The income from my teaching job was the only way we could make ends meet."

"Maybe I'll need to take a second job, too," said
Eva. "It would be worth it, to have times like this."

"Well," said Mom, standing up and brushing
dirt from her knees, "it's time to get ready for
our picnic."

Eva and Ingrid made sandwiches and packed
the picnic. Then the family headed to the pond.
"You want to race to the pond like we
used to?" Eva asked Ingrid.

Ingrid laughed and said, "No, not today. It's too hot." Then she added, "I'm not going to stay at the pond very long, Eva. I've got a lot of work to do preparing my senior project."

"You've got lots of time to plan your project! School doesn't start for more than two months! It's just an afternoon," Eva shot back. She sounded like she was going to cry.

"This project's important, Eva," Ingrid replied softly. "I have a lot of research and planning to do if I want it to turn out well. I'm graduating next year. Having good grades will help me get the job I want."

"Why can't you stay here and work on the dairy farm after you graduate? What's wrong with that?" demanded Eva.

"Nothing's wrong with that," said Ingrid, "but I don't want to be a dairy farmer. It's a great choice for some people, but not for me. I'm getting a degree in business. I want to try something different."

"You're planning on leaving the farm?" asked Eva in disbelief.

"That's not what I said," answered Ingrid. "I love our farm. But you heard Mom. There's not always enough money to pay the bills. I want to figure out a way for our farm to make money."

"Why can't we just let things stay the way they are?" asked Eva, with a childlike pout.

"If Mom and Dad owed too much money, they'd probably need to sell some land to pay off their debts," explained Ingrid. "If that happened, there might not be enough land left to keep a dairy farm going."

"We could lose the farm?" asked Eva, her voice trembling.

"I didn't say that's going to happen," Ingrid said in a soothing voice. "Mom and Dad aren't about to sell the farm. I just don't want things to get to the point where we have to. I'm trying to think of a solution before there's a serious problem."

When they got to the pond, they spread a tablecloth on the picnic table. They laid out sandwiches and drinks. Egg salad sandwiches were her favorite, but Eva no longer felt hungry. She was silent as everyone chattered away. Then Dad and Ryan started throwing a Frisbee, and Ingrid and Mom were talking about Ingrid's project. She couldn't help feeling that something important had been taken away from her.

Eva looked across the pond at the row of trees at the fence line, separating their farm from their neighbor's. She walked down to the pond and skipped a few stones. These hundred acres of pasture and woods and cows were her whole world. She bit her lip. There were ducks on the pond, and the sky was a perfect summer blue. She couldn't believe that everything could look so right and not be that way.

When Eva started back to the picnic table, she saw Ingrid walking back to the house. Dad and Ryan were still throwing the Frisbee, so Eva took the opportunity to talk to her mom, who was sitting at the picnic table.

"Mom, can I ask you something?" Eva blurted out. "We have more cows now than we used to. We must be getting lots more milk. Why aren't we making more money?"

Her mother looked affectionately at her. She understood exactly what Eva had been thinking. "The expense of running a farm increases each year, but the price of milk hasn't risen the same way," her mother said slowly and clearly. "Milk prices fluctuate—they go up and down. But they never go up enough. So our income from milk sales is getting smaller," she explained.

"If our expenses get too big, will we have to sell the farm?" Eva asked, tears welling in her eyes.

"It's not something we want to do," said Mom. "You know, when Dad and I were growing up, there were lots of small farms here in Ohio. We thought they'd always be here. But over the years, most of them have disappeared. Sometimes families sold their farms to **developers,** who built houses or businesses on them. Sometimes bigger farms buy the small farms. Now those large farms are making most of the profit, and the small farms are dying away."

Dad and Ryan had returned to the table while Mom was talking. Dad spoke up firmly, "Don't worry, Pumpkin, we'll never sell the farm. My great-grandparents started this farm. It's going to be here for you, Ryan, and Ingrid. We're not going to let anything happen to it."

Eva wanted to believe Dad's reassuring words, but maybe, she thought, the farm wouldn't always be theirs.

developers – people who buy areas of land, build houses or businesses on it, and then sell the buildings for profit

Eva's Diary

June 23, 2002

I thought this summer was going to be fun, but now I'm worried that we might lose our farm! Today I found out that our farm is making less and less money. Sometimes there isn't enough to pay all our bills! I know we don't have lots of money, but I always thought we had enough. I guess I never really thought about it much. Dad says not to worry, but I am worried.

When we left the pond, Mom said that maybe we should all think of different ways to make the farm profitable. After all, Ingrid's studying business, and Ryan's taking some agricultural courses at college. Dad told Mom that the way they ran the farm was between them. Then Mom said that she thought Ingrid, Ryan, and I have every right to be involved in making the farm work if it's going to be ours one day. Boy, was it a tense walk back to the house!

Later I heard Mom and Dad arguing. I couldn't hear what they were saying, but I think it was about whether or not to tell us how bad things are.

Sometimes You Need to Cry

I n September, Ingrid and Ryan returned to college, their mother resumed teaching, and Eva started eighth grade. In October there was a stretch of warm, sunny days when the sky shone a clear turquoise blue. *It's like summer's saying, "Remember what I'm like. I'm going away for a while, but I'll be back again,"* thought Eva.

When Eva and her mom arrived home after school on one of those glorious October afternoons, Dad announced that he was going to start baling the hay they'd cut and dried. "The weather forecast doesn't look too good for the upcoming weekend. I want to get the hay baled and stored before then," Dad said. "Can you two handle the milking? That way, I might be able to get the rest of the baling done this afternoon. Then I can load and store the bales tomorrow. This could well be the last chance I have to get more hay ready for winter storage. There's no sense in letting rain spoil our hay."

"Just be back before dark," said Mom.

"Oh, of course," grinned Dad as he started the tractor. "I never miss dinner."

Eva and her mom worked steadily, milking and feeding the cows. Not until they were done did they notice that dusk had fallen.

"Dad should be back any time now," said Eva as they headed out of the barn.

Ten minutes later it was dark. Mom tried Dad on her cell phone but got no answer. Then she tried him again.

"He probably doesn't hear it ringing with the baler going," said Eva.

"He shouldn't be using the baler at night. The ground's too uneven to operate that machinery in the dark. If it gets stuck in a rut, the tractor and baler could topple over," said Mom.

Eva felt her mouth go dry. "Dad's used the baler hundreds of times. Maybe the tractor's run out of gas or the baler broke down, and Dad's walking back."

Mom chewed her lip. "Come on, Eva, get in the pickup truck. We're going to get Dad."

Mom headed down the dirt track to the distant field where Dad was supposed to be baling hay. As the truck bounced along, Eva felt her stomach clench. Why hadn't they met Dad on his way back?

Suddenly, relief swept over her. "Over there!
I see the glow from the headlights."

As Mom drove toward the glow, Eva's feeling
of relief began to fade. Why weren't the headlights
from Dad's tractor moving? Had something
broken down?

Soon the pickup truck's headlights swept over
the tractor and the baler. Eva smothered a cry.
The tractor and the baler were flipped onto their
sides, but where was Dad?

Mom cut the engine and Eva ran out of the
pickup toward the toppled machinery. "Dad,
Dad!" she cried. "Where are you?"

Then she saw the motionless shape of her
father. The baler was lying across Dad, hiding his
legs from view. "Mom, quick! He's over here!"

Eva heard Mom calling for an ambulance.
Then she said, "Eva, take the flashlight from
the glove box and run back to the house. When
the ambulance and the fire department arrive,
tell them where we are. I'll stay here with Dad."

Too stunned to answer, Eva nodded and
stumbled back along the dirt track to the house,
running as fast as she could. She arrived seconds
before the ambulance and rescue workers drove

up to the house. Eva flagged them down and climbed inside the rescue truck. She directed the driver to the accident.

After they arrived at the scene, everything was a blur. Soon lights from the rescue vehicles brightened the scene of the wreckage. Comments flew around Eva and her mother as rescue workers struggled to free Dad from under the weight of the baling machine.

"He's unconscious but alive."

"Keep him immobilized. His neck and spine might be injured."

"Steady, steady."

Mom held Eva tight as they stood away from the workers. A police officer came, and Mom answered questions. The officer urged Mom and Eva to return to the house. He promised the ambulance would pick up Mom so she could go to the hospital with Dad.

Back home, Mom called Ingrid and Ryan and told them what had happened. She called her sister Pat too.

"Aunt Pat's coming over right away," said Mom. "She'll bring you to the hospital. I'm going to ride with Dad in the ambulance."

"Is Dad going to be all right?" asked Eva shakily.

"I hope so, but I don't know," answered Mom helplessly.

Within minutes, the red light of the ambulance streamed through the kitchen window. Mom rushed out and disappeared through the open doors at the back of the ambulance. Eva saw the rigid shape of her father. He was strapped to the stretcher. *Please let him be all right,* she thought.

As soon as Aunt Pat arrived, she gave Eva a great big hug. Eva grabbed a coat, and they started to the hospital. *Why did this have to happen?* wondered Eva silently as she clenched her fists and struggled not to cry, peering out the window into the darkness.

"It's okay to cry, honey," came Aunt Pat's kind voice. "Sometimes you just need to cry. Go ahead, there's a box of tissues on the seat between us."

The tears flooded down Eva's cheeks and sobs wracked her body. By the time they reached the hospital, the tears had stopped.

"Better bring the tissues," said Aunt Pat.

Eva spotted her mom, looking pale and drawn, in the busy emergency room. Eva flung her arms around her mother and asked, "Is Daddy all right?"

"The doctors are operating on him now," she replied, holding Eva tightly.

He was still in the operating room when Ingrid and Ryan arrived at the hospital. By then Eva had a terrible headache, and the same question kept pounding in her head. *What,* she wondered, *will happen to us if Dad doesn't make it?*

Eva's Diary

October 17, 2002

Yesterday turned into the worst kind of day. From now on, on every October 16, I'll remember Dad's accident. Mom said the baler probably got caught in a rut and tipped over. As it tipped, so did the tractor. Dad got pinned beneath the baler.

Last night was the longest I can ever remember. Dad was in surgery for more than five hours. Then Dad went to the Intensive Care Unit, or ICU. We took turns going to see him. He was unconscious. He was so still. An oxygen mask covered his nose and mouth, and tubes led from different machines to his arms. I whispered, "Dad, it's me, Eva. I love you." I kissed his cheek. I don't know if he heard me, but I felt better telling him.

We still don't know if Dad is going to be OK. The doctors aren't sure yet whether his spinal cord is damaged. If it is, Dad might not be able to walk—or even move—ever again.

Mom and Aunt Pat left for the hospital early this morning. Ryan, Ingrid, and I stayed here to milk and feed the cows. We're going to the hospital now. I hope Dad will be OK. I'm afraid. I don't want him to die.

Home Again

"Let's put the couch over in the bay window. Eva, put the other end table next to the couch. That way, Mom and Dad can use this corner as a sitting room. Now, let's put the bed along the wall where the couch was. Put the dresser where the bookcase stood," said Ingrid. She was directing her siblings in turning the downstairs living room into a bedroom.

It took another hour before they were done. Mom looked in from the office where she was paying bills. "What would I do without you?" she asked, smiling.

"It's hard to believe that Dad's finally coming home from the hospital today," said Ryan.

Ryan's good-natured disposition reminded Eva of their dad. At least, the way he was before the accident. Eva wondered if Dad would keep that cheerful way of looking at things after all he'd been through. But she didn't say that.

"Just in time for New Year's Eve," added Eva.

"It'll be good to start the new year together," said Mom thoughtfully.

"It's got to be better than the last part of this year's been," said Eva. She was thinking back over the five weeks her father had spent in the ICU. Mom had taken a leave of absence from her job so that she could be with Dad. Ryan had insisted on withdrawing from his classes so that he could stay home and help with the farm. Then came the weeks Dad spent at the rehabilitation center. He had to build up his muscles and slowly learn how to walk again. Now, at last, he was coming home.

"The doctor said it's going to be hard. It's going to take a lot of time and lots of physical therapy before Dad's strong again. He won't be able to do the things he's been used to doing," explained Mom.

"At least his broken bones are healing well. We're going to have to help him with the rest," Ingrid said. Her blue eyes looked calmly and clearly into the future, as if she could see what was coming.

"Yes, his body is healing," said Mom, "but Dad's going to be angry that he's not allowed to do the things he used to do. The doctor warned Dad that it could take up to six months before he can walk up and down stairs and be able to do chores."

"We'll be here to keep him company when you start teaching again," said Ingrid, "at least for a few weeks. School doesn't start for us until the end of January."

"That will be a big help," said Mom. "Oh! Look at the time! Eva, are you coming with me to pick up Dad? We'd better get going."

As they drove to the hospital, Mom shared her thoughts with Eva. "Last summer Dad and I talked about whether I should give up my job and start working full time on the farm.

He wanted us to buy a few more cows. We couldn't take care of any more by ourselves, but we couldn't afford to hire anyone to help. The only option was for me to quit my job," she began.

Eva swallowed hard and thanked her lucky stars that Mom had not quit her job.

"The catch was, if I left my job, we'd lose our health insurance. We decided we couldn't risk it. It's a good thing, huh?" she said, shaking her head.

When they arrived at the hospital, Dad was waiting in the reception area. Eva ran to him and hugged him. "I'm so glad you're coming home, Dad," she smiled.

"So am I, Pumpkin," said Dad. He refused a wheelchair to get to the car. He struggled to make his way on crutches. By the time they got there, his face was drawn and pinched.

"Does it hurt a lot, Dad?" asked Eva.

"You could say that," he answered, "but if I don't walk, I'll be in a wheelchair. And that's something I don't want. It would be hard to do the chores."

"Russ, the doctor said ... " began Mom.

"Kathy, I know what the doctor said. I don't want to talk about that right now. Can't it wait?" replied Dad sharply.

They drove home in silence. Eva cringed
inwardly as Dad strained getting out of the car. He
refused Ryan's offer of a helping hand and silently
made his way into the house.

"Welcome home, Dad," said Ingrid as she
hugged him.

"It's good to be home," said Dad, making an effort to smile. "It smells good. I could use some home cooking."

"It's New Year's Eve," said Eva. "We're having a special dinner so we can say goodbye to the old year and welcome the new one."

"It'll be good riddance to this year, that's for sure," said Dad sourly. "Do I have time for a quick nap before dinner?"

"Sure, Dad," said Ingrid. "We set up a bedroom downstairs for you and Mom, so you don't have to climb the stairs for a while. It's where the living room was."

"I'll find it," said Dad as he headed out of the kitchen.

Dad looked refreshed after his nap, and dinner started out as a cheerful meal. "It really is good to be home," said Dad. He looked at them all and at the streamers and "Welcome Home" banner that decorated the kitchen. "When are you all heading back to school?" asked Dad.

"School starts for Eva and me next Monday," said Mom.

"I will be going back at the end of January," added Ingrid.

Ryan hesitated a moment, then announced, "I've decided not to go back this year. I'm taking a leave of absence so I can help out with the farm."

Slowly Dad put down his fork. "I don't think that's a good idea. You should go back to school. We'll manage just fine."

Mom said, "Ryan, you should think about this carefully. You need to think about your future."

"I *am* thinking about my future," said Ryan. "I need to be here right now, helping on the farm. You need three people to do the chores, and Dad can't do them now. It's too much for you and Eva to do everything yourselves."

"Ryan, if you believe my doctor, I might never again be able to do chores," said Dad. "So don't give up your education for something that you don't want to do."

Eva held her breath as Ryan said, "I'm not sure what I want to do for the long term. But I do know that I want us to keep the farm. If I'm not here to help, we may lose the farm. Then I may never have a chance to be a dairy farmer. I'd rather work now to save the farm."

"There might not be enough money anyway to pay the bills. I've been thinking about this since the accident. We're not making nearly as much as we need to make to pay our bills. And since my accident, we have more bills than ever. Frankly, we should sell the place," growled Dad. "That would be easier for everyone."

"Sell the farm! You've got to be joking!" cried Mom. Her calm face turned into a mass of lines and scowls.

"Dad, no!" cried Eva as Ryan and Ingrid looked at their father in disbelief.

"Why not?" asked Dad. "It's a burden to all of you. I can't help out now. And who knows when I'll be able to work again? You've seen how slow I am on these crutches. At the moment, I'm a useless wreck of a man."

"It is not a burden to all of us!" retorted Eva. "I love the farm. So do Ryan and Ingrid. They may not want to be dairy farmers, but I do."

"Russ, please don't give up now! Not after everything you've been through," begged his wife, trying to calm herself down. "Our children love the farm, and so do I. We're not willing to give it up. Let's start the new year thinking about what we can do, not what we can't do."

Eva's Diary

December 31, 2002

What a New Year's Eve this has turned out to be!
I couldn't believe it when Dad said we should sell the farm. I wanted to yell at him to stop feeling so sorry for himself. At least he's still alive, and he's got all of us. We all love the farm as much as he does, but maybe some of us love it in different ways. I didn't want to hurt Dad's feelings, so I didn't tell him everything I was thinking.
I think he's going to listen to us. I know (at least I hope) we can convince him to keep the farm and not give up.

CHAPTER 4

January 2003

Time to Heal

A few weeks later, Mom decided it was time to talk about the future of the farm. After dinner, they cleared the dishes and gathered at the kitchen table. Mom sat at the head of the table, facing her husband at the other end.

"Russ, while you were in the hospital we began thinking of ways to change our farm business and make it more profitable. I think we have come up with a few ideas," Mom said. "For several years we've been focusing on making our dairy herd bigger. But we haven't seen any profit. We need to improve the way we run the farm before we think about getting bigger. I think we can save some money if we change the way we do things."

Russ stared at his wife. "So what do you think we should do? We can't cut back on feed, or the cows won't produce milk. A cow can eat from 40 pounds to 80 pounds of food a day!"

"I'm not saying that we should stop feeding our cows. Maybe instead of buying expensive feed from the farm suppliers, we should grow as much of the cows' feed as we can. We have plenty of pasture filled with nutritious grasses. Ryan and I have done research on how to cut feed costs. Ryan, why don't you tell Dad about it?"

"Basically, in our plan, the cows are moved through a series of grass pastures, grazing as they go along. They graze in a couple of pastures until it's time to move them into fresh ones where the grass is taller. We'll keep an eye on the grass so that it doesn't get too short when the cows are grazing. That way the grass will grow back quickly. When the grass is at the right height, we'll move the cows to the next pasture. It's an environmentally friendly way of spreading manure, too," explained Ryan.

"Won't it cost a lot to build these pastures?" quizzed Dad.

"No. We'll use electrical fencing. It's easy to put up, and we can move it around if we need to," answered Ryan. "Another problem," he continued, "is that we spend a lot of money on medicines to keep the cows healthy. Our vet bills are huge. We can cut out some of that expense by making our farm more **organic.** People and businesses will pay more money for milk that comes from cows fed on natural grass and is free of antibiotics and medicines.

"The idea is," said Ingrid, "that our cows may produce less milk, but we will get more money for the milk. This will cut costs on feed and vet bills."

Eva could see that Ingrid's way of putting things simply was starting to interest Dad. But he was still glaring at them. Eva knew that her dad felt ganged up on. But she didn't know how to make him feel more a part of things.

---

organic – produced without chemicals, antibiotics, or pesticides

Before she could say anything, her mother jumped back in.

"We'll have to spend time on new chores, like growing grass and other crops to feed the cows during the winter. Sure, we'll have to buy some feed, but nothing like the quantities we've been buying," Mom said.

"It costs money to do all the things you're talking about. Where are we going to get it?" Dad asked.

Mom answered, "We still have some savings. And I am going to apply for a loan."

"A loan? How could we get a loan?" asked Dad. "We've got a farm that's barely scraping by, and I can't work. We have two grown children who might decide to take paying jobs or go back to college, and one child who's still in school. And we don't even have enough money to hire part-time help."

Mom glared at Dad. "You've forgotten to mention the things we do have. We have land, cows, equipment, and a house. We also have three determined children who have already put a lot of time and effort into thinking of ways to save this farm."

Just then, the phone rang. Eva jumped up to get it. "Mom, it's Aunt Pat."

"Can I call her back?" her mom said.

Eva took a deep breath. She covered the phone with her hand, and said, as forcefully as she could, "No, she needs to talk to you now." It was a lie, of course, but she thought her dad might explode if they pushed their case any harder.

While her mom was on the phone, Eva called Ingrid into the living room. "Ingrid, we're pushing Dad too hard," she whispered. "You've got to do something."

Ingrid looked at her little sister. Eva's good sense of people, and especially their dad, was absolutely on the mark. She looked into her sister's face and said, "Oh, Eva, you are right." Then she hugged her and said, "Good going!"

When their mother got off the phone a few minutes later, Ingrid and Eva were washing the dishes. Ryan and their dad were watching a basketball game on TV.

"Where is everybody?" her mother asked.

"Chilling out," Ingrid said. "We decided that Dad was on information overload. Eva was smart enough to figure that out while we were so busy lecturing him."

Mom started to frown, but then she looked at her youngest child and her face broke into a smile. "Eva, you're so right. I was just too intense. Thank you, dear. You understand your dad really well!"

While Ingrid and Eva finished the dishes, their mom sat down in the kitchen. Soon Dad and Ryan came back to the table.

"Well," Dad said, slowly easing himself into his place at the kitchen table, "I guess we didn't quite finish this discussion. Ryan explained a few things to me while we were watching the game. He told me about the ideas for processing and bottling our own milk and cream. He said we could even make yogurt. He mentioned the research Ingrid has done surveying restaurants and local people about buying these products. It's a lot for me to think about."

"If we decide to have an on-farm processing and bottling plant, I can get some of my friends to help me fix up the old barn," Ryan broke in. "I'm sure I can learn to work and maintain a processing plant. You know how I love machinery."

"Maybe we could make ice cream and open an ice-cream stand," piped up Eva. "Lots of people go out for ice cream in the summer."

"You know, I just worry that we could lose the things that are worth keeping if we can't repay the loan," countered Dad. Then he stopped and looked at his family. "I guess you all love the farm as much as I always have. Maybe you're right. It's time to make some changes and fight to keep what we have. How should we get started?"

Eva's Diary

January 24, 2003

It may sound strange to say this, because you know how much I hate arguments, but I'm glad that the four of us challenged Dad. It gave Dad a chance to see how much we all love the farm and how much we want to keep it. We also proved to him that we had thought about ways to keep the farm.

Dad's been more like his old self ever since he learned how much we all care about our home. He has even started keeping the records and paying the bills. He said he might as well use his hands and brain while his legs are getting back into shape. And when he smiled and winked at Mom yesterday, I knew that everything was going to be all right.

We're in This Together

Eva finished restocking the refrigerator in the dairy store and smiled as Dad rang up the last customer's purchases.

"You have a good day, Erma, and tell Fred to stop by some time. We have a calf he might be interested in taking a look at," said Dad.

"I'll do that, Russ. It is a wonder what you have been able to do with this place."

Dad smiled. "It wasn't me. It was this industrious family of mine. You know, Erma, I never thought things could be this good."

Eva looked at her dad standing behind the cash register, his tanned face beaming. It had been more than two-and-a-half years since Dad had returned home from the hospital, pale, gaunt, weak, and angry.

"When I got home from the hospital, Erma, I thought we were going to have to sell part of the land. We had so many bills to pay for the equipment we needed. But Ingrid came to the rescue. As part of her senior project at college, she prepared a business plan that described in detail the kind of business we wanted to set up here. She wrote a marketing plan and figured out who our customers would be."

"But, Russ," Erma said, "didn't this all cost a lot of money?"

"Well, Erma, the answer is yes and no. Ingrid figured out how to finance the operation and how the business was going to be run. She surveyed local businesses and restaurants to find out what kind of dairy products they wanted. Ingrid did an incredible job. I was so proud of her. But the business plan wasn't enough. When we showed the plan to local banks, they turned us down flat. They said the business was too risky."

"That's what I would have expected,"
Erma said.

"We just had to go to plan number two,
Erma. Ingrid heard that the state government
was awarding grants to people who wanted to
start new agricultural businesses. She applied
for a grant. She explained how we wanted to
change our traditional family dairy farm into a
different type of family business. The State
Agricultural Department was impressed with
the application. They even sent a man out to
look over the farm. In the end they awarded us
a small grant."

Erma nodded her head. "Was that all the
money you needed?"

"No," said Dad, "but the agricultural grant
made the local banks take another look at our
business plan."

"Do you remember the day you took the call
from the bank, Dad?" Eva prompted him.

"Oh yeah, a couple of restaurants and a
store had sent Ingrid letters asking when she
could start delivering farm-fresh milk."

"So Mom sent the letters to a couple of the
banks, just to prove that there was serious

interest in the farm products we wanted to sell," Eva added.

"The day the call came saying we'd gotten the loan, I let out a yell so loud that a chunk of plaster fell down from the ceiling," said Russ.

Eva giggled at her dad's exaggeration.

"Then everything else fell into place," said Russ. "Ryan and Ingrid visited some small family-owned processing and bottling operations to learn how they ran their operations. Now, it's all history, Erma. We bottle our own milk and cream and make butter once a week."

"Luckily, Ingrid and Mom took my advice about having an ice-cream stand," said Eva. "They took a course to learn how to make ice cream."

"And you make the best ice cream in the county," said Erma. "I am so glad everything has worked out. After your accident, I was worried about your family and your farm."

"Well, Erma, I appreciate that. But, um, if you don't have to rush off, there is a lot more to this story."

Erma laughed. "You go right ahead. Eva, run and get me an ice cream while I listen to your dad."

"Remember when this building was one of our barns? Ryan converted the barn into a processing and bottling operation. The cows are milked at one end of the barn, and the milk is processed and bottled on the other side of that wall. Then Ryan and his friends put up a divider and turned the front portion of the processing and bottling barn into the Peterson's Dairy Store. Do you like it?"

"I love it," said Erma. "And I love this ice cream. Thank you, Eva. What do I owe you for it?"

"Nothing," said Russ. "You listened to me brag about my family. That's payment enough."

Erma laughed and said, "Thanks, Russ. I'll see you soon."

When Erma left, Dad limped over to Eva and put his arm around her. "Look at it all. I might not be doing the things I did a couple of years ago, but you know, Pumpkin, I think maybe everything's turned out for the best. In fact, I'm sure of it."

Eva's Diary

August 6, 2005

I never thought I'd say this, but I sure am glad that Ingrid went to college and studied business! I don't know if we'd still have the farm without her.

It's amazing how many people come here each day in summer to get ice cream, especially on weekends! I can't help feeling proud about that, since it was my idea to have the ice-cream stand. I wanted to crow like a rooster when we sold out the first weekend the stand opened!

People like looking at the cows, too, and seeing them grazing in the fields. One woman told me that seeing a farm like ours reminds her of her farm when she was a kid.

It's good to see Mom and Dad smiling again. My favorite part of every day, though, is going out to see the cows with Dad. There's a lot he can't do, but he has made so many changes. He's really proud that we've been able to keep the farm. I know he's happy that we're all working together on our dairy farm, and so am I.

Farm Life in the Midwest

The land of the midwestern states is very fertile. There are many farms growing many different kinds of food. Some farms grow crops. Crops are plants that are grown for people to use, such as food. The main crops in the Midwest are wheat and corn. Other farms raise animals for food. Pigs and cattle are raised for meat. Cattle are also raised for their milk.

Dairy Farming

Cows that produce milk are raised on a dairy farm. The word *dairy* refers to any products made from milk. Butter, cheese, yogurt, and ice cream are all made from the milk we get from cows. One dairy cow can produce about 1,800 gallons (6,814 liters) of milk a year.

Farm Sizes

Dairy farms come in different sizes. Some farms are small. They usually have just a small amount of land and raise a small herd of cows. Small farms are often owned by a family. There are also very large farms. They have large amounts of land and raise many cows. Large farms are like factories. They use many machines to help raise and milk the cows.

Organic Dairy Farming

Most dairy farms today rely on science to help them produce more milk. The cows are fed specially-made food to help them stay healthy and grow. They are also given drugs called hormones and steroids. These drugs help the cows to produce more milk. Some farmers do not want to use special feeds and medicines. They prefer to allow their cows to eat grass in pastures and produce milk in a natural way. This type of farming is called organic farming.

Write a Personal Letter

In the story, Eva and her family are facing a time of challenge and change. Imagine that you are Eva's friend and you are going to write her a letter.

- Copy the chart below.

- In the first column, list some of the challenges Eva and her family are facing in the story.

- In the second column, list possible ways to face these challenges. Use information from the story as well as other sources.

- Use your completed chart to write a letter to Eva. Offer your advice and encouragement to help her deal with the challenges she faces.

Challenge	Ways to face the problem
1. Eva's family needs to make the farm more profitable.	1. They can make their farm organic.

Read More About the Midwest

Find and read more books about the Midwest. As you read, think about these questions. They will help you understand more about this topic.

- What are the midwestern states?

- What are some of the cultures and traditions found in the Midwest?

- What are some of the important industries in the Midwest region?

- What are some natural resources found in the Midwest?

- What are some physical features of the Midwest landscape?

SUGGESTED READING
Reading Expeditions
Readings About America:
The Midwest Today

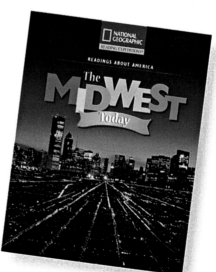